Start to Learn
Words

Green Android

Created and produced by:
Green Android Ltd
49 Beaumont Court
Upper Clapton Road
London E5 8BG
United Kingdom
www.greenandroid.co.uk

ISBN 978-1-909244-05-4

Copyright © Green Android Ltd 2013

Acknowledgements

Images © dreamstime.com: hose © Fibobjects; go-kart © Jaggat; Truck races, helicopter © Martinased; hand © aidaricci.

Images © fotolia.com: ambulance © Robert Asento; ants © Henrik Larsson; apron, cushion © Kayros Studio; aubergine, chocolate, pancakes, pomegranate © Natika; avocado © atoss; balloons © Aleks_ei; bananas © Nikolai Sorokin; bathrobe © Volha Ahranovich; beachbag © by-studio; beans © Joanna Glab; beetles © Inzyx; biplane © plentius; blueberries © Mariusz Blach; boiled egg © dusk; boots © Angel Simon; bottles © picsfive; boy in hat and gloves © Sergiy Bykhunenko; boy on scooter © Szasz-Fabian Erika; brocolli © Christian Jung; brussels sprouts © andriigorulko; bucket © savage ultralight; building bricks © atm2003; bulldozer © raulsagredo; butterflies © Tatesh, Marco Uliana; buttons © DOC RABE Media, pzAxe; cabbage © Sport Moments; calfs © sherjaca; cardigan, sweater, woolly hat © Ruslan Kudrin; carpenter, waiter © Kurhan; carrots © Dionisvera; cauliflower, straw bale © Elena Schweitzer; chicken © Jacek Chabraszewski; chicks, tree frog © Sascha Burkard; chimpanzee, corn snake © Eric Isselée; comb © terex; combine harvesting © Kletr; cookie cutter © lantapix; cow © lightpoet; crab © a9luha; croissant © robynmac; cup of Coffee © Graham Kidd Zenith; cupcakes © Ruth Black; deawers © Paul Maguire; dinosaur © morchella; doctor, nurse © Minerva Studio; doll © amorfati.art; dollhouse © mariesacha; donuts © Nitr; drum © Winston Link; duck, ducklings, goose, sticks © DenisNata; dump truck © nikitos77; excavator © Gudellaphoto; farm animal toys © Brocreative; field © Elenathewise; Fireman © Luis Louro; flower © Brilt, Digitalpress, iLight foto, novadomus, Smileus, tr3gi, terex, Yeko Photo Studio; football © Smileus; forklift truck © art_zzz; frame © ihorzigor; french fries © Peter Polak; gardening tools © rineca; go-kart © Jaggat; goat © cynoclub; Grater © Andrey Savin; hair brush, motorbike © cristi180884; hand © aidaricci; hand puppet © Dmitriy Kalinin; helicopter © Martinspurny; hen © sval7; hose © Fibobjects; hot-air balloon © beachboyx10, Tof Locoste; ice lollies © graja, unpict; jacket © Roman Sigaev; jams © Rafa Irusta; jeep, vest © pzAxe; kangaroo © anankkml; kiwi fruit © Zbigniew Janusz Koby; knickers © Khvost; koala © daphot75; lamp © honda vita; leaf © alexfiodorov; leggings © Liaurinko; lettuce © Aaron Amat; mare and Foal © ssspablo; milkshakes © Little_wine_fly; motor scooter © F.Schmidt; mouse © Vera Kuttelvaserova; muffin © Smart7; musician © rtranq; noodles, waffles, yogurt with raspberries © Africa Studio; Orange © Vidady; oven glove © matka_Wariatka; pan © vnlit; party hats © Lucky Dragon; passion fruit © Sandy Schulze; pasta salad © victoria p.; Pear © Ahmad Affzan; pepper © Kenishirotie; pig © Anatolii; police car © frog-travel; policeman © Lisa F. Young; pumpkin © Jacek Fulawka; rabbit © Oleg Zhukov; raspberries © Mny-Jhee; rice © oriori; roadsign © rnl; roadtrain © HenningManning; robot © Proto1138; rubber duck © Britta Laser, ctvvelve; sailboat © Marina Ignatova; schoolbus © rgbspace; sea © Pakhnyushchy; sea lion © Springfield Gallery; seashells © viktoriya89; shorts © Worakit Sirijinda; skateboard © Phattman; skirt © Coprid; snail © Pampalini; soap © Atiketta Sangasaeng; soup © rimglow; speedboat © Angelo Giampiccolo; swim ring © Cristiano Ribeiro; tiger © davidevison; toilet © MarFot; toilet paper © mariocigic; tomatoes © Anna Kucherova; toothpaste © Mau Horng; toy car © Aleksandr Ugorenkov, Amore, Larisa Epor; toy train © Justinb; tractor and plough © toshi8; train © Scanrail; tram © Pixel & Création; tree (seasons) © ivan kmit; trousers © windu; truck © Martinased; turkey © Irina Khomenko; TV © AKS; water © seen.

Images © istock: baby © jfairone.

Images © shutterstock.com: african American boy © Harm Kruyshaar; airbus © Kosorukov Dmitry; airship © totophotos; alligator, camel, kennel, seagull © Eric Isselee; american Football © Denis Pepin; ants © Andrey Pavlov; apples © Albo003, cloki, Valentyn Volkov; babies © aporokh at gmail dot com, Paul Hakimata Photography, Denys Kurbatov; backpack © Mike Flippo; bagel © Sally Scott; baked potato © Timolina; ballerina © Yuganov Konstantin; bananas © Maks Narodenko; Baseball © Alex Staroseltsev; beach ball © koosen; Bearded Dragon © tratong; bed © Chukcha; belt © Marko Poplasen; binoculars © Ratana21; bison, gorilla © Aaron Amat; blocks © Eillen; board game © Tatik22; boat © Modfos; border collie © Erik Lam; bowls, skittles, feathers, orange © Africa Studio; boy eating cornflakes © Noam Armonn; boy in pijama © matka_Wariatka; boy on bike © Paul Vasarhelyi; Boy wih a dog © Andresr; boy with knife and fork © grafvision; boy with toothbrush © Carlos Horta; boys © Andresr, caldix, Felix Mizioznikov, Karen H. Ilagan, Tom Wang, Michel Borges, YanLev; Bread © Artur Synenko; broom © terekhov igor; brown bear © Artem Illarionov; brown sugar © Diana Taliun; Bubble Bath © Michael C. Gray; building block tower © c12; bunting © Andrea Slatter; bush © Johannes Kornelius; butterfly © Aleksandr Kurganov, chungking; camera © Anastasios Kandris; candles © Maria Meester, mrsnstudio, Fanfo; cap, cardboard box © windu; carpenter © auremar; cash register © Robert Cernohlavek; cereal, kettle, money © Kitch Bain; chair and table © Kletr; chalkboard © Sarunyu_foto; chalks © de2marco; cheese © Valentina Razumova; cheetah © Arnoud Quanjer; chef © michaeljung; cherries © Pakhnyushcha; child`s clothes © Vasina Natalia; coal © Geo-grafika; colander © Shawn Hempel; compact car © DDCoral; computer © Igor Klimov; container ship © Gary Blakeley; cooker © Neamov; cookies © Dmitrij Skorobogatov, endeavor, Sergio33; corn cob © Roxana Bashyrova; courgettes © MichaelJayBerlin; courier, deckchair, gardener © Andrey_Popov; crayons © Lucie Lang; crocodile © Anan Kaewkhammul; cucumber © Viktar Malyshchyts;cup of tea, starfish © Galushko Sergey; daffodil © MarFot; dandelion © Nancy Kennedy; dinosaur © BORTEL Pavel - Pavelmidi; dirty football, teddy © Picsfive; discus fish © Ekaterina V. Borisova; door © ollyy; ear-muffs © Evgenia Bolyukh; earthworm © iliuta goean; egg in pan © HomeArt; elephant, dolphin © Four Oaks; envelope © Litvinenko Anastasia; eraser © Blinka; exercise book © Falkiewicz Henryk; felt-tip pens © artproem; fence © Dr. Cloud; flower © Cosmin Manci, Hong Vo, Roman Sigaev, tr3gin, Yeko Photo Studio; flower pots © Quang Ho; flying sparrow © Protasov AN; Football © Olga Popova; footballer © RTimages; fox © Menno Schaefer; frog © SantiPhotoSS; gardening fork © Claudio Baldini; gardening gloves © Richard Peterson; gate © Madeleine Forsberg; gazelle © Fotomicar; gift, gift boxes, guitar, nuts © Elena Schweitzer; giraffe © Johan Swanepoel; girl © Batyreva Irina, BlueOrange Studio, Elena Schweitzer, Eskymaks, Jaimie Duplass, Kalmatsuy Tatyana, Michael Pettigrew, Simone van den Berg; girl eats fruit salad © Serhiy Kobyakov; girl on swing © 2xSamara.com; girl with pinwheel © Kravchenko Marina; girl with umbrella © StockLite; glider © zentilia; globe © Hurst Photo; glue © alejandro dans neergaard; glue stick © Alexandr Makarov; goat kid, wool © oksana2010; grapes, milk © Evgeny Karandaev; graph paper © optimarc; grass © lazybuffy; hands © inxti; hang-glider © Elena Koulik; hanging decoration © Anteromite; hippopotamus © alexsvirid; hoody © Nadezda Cruzova; hotrod © Barry Blackburn; humpback whale © Claude Huot; jacket © Karkas; jeans © Roman Sigaev; jetski © Crok Photography; Jigsaw © STILLFX; kitchen scales © Valeriy Ivashchenko; kite © Piotr Sikora; kittens © Bartkowski; ladybird © Serg64; leaves © Nik Merkulov, Triff, zhangyang13576997233; lemon © DenisNata; limousine © LesPalenik; lion © Aaron Amat; long and short pencils © HomeStudio; lunchbox, vase © Ivonne Wierink; magnet © James Steidl; magnifying glass © jcjgphotography; man (back and front) © Tom Wang; marbles © Kristof Degreef; marker pen © Luminis; mechanic © Dmitry Kalinovsky; meerkat © AnetaPics; monorail © gkuna; monster truck © Natursports; moon decorations © HamsterMan, Edyta Pawlowska; moose © Wesley Aston; mugs © area381; mushrooms © Laborant; nail brush © Rick P Lewis; notebook © Garsya; onion © Denis Sokolov; orange juice © FCG; painter © vita khorzhevska; panda, potato, vet © leungchopan; park bench © liveostockimages; peach © Dudarev Mikhail; peas © ravl; pencil-case © robootb; penguins © kwest; picture frame © Blacknote; pig © dyoma; pilot © wavebreakmedia; pine cones © Sony Ho; pineapple © Andrii Gorulko, volff; pink feathers © nito; pizza slice © Iurii Konoval; plant © great_photos; playground slide © Sergiy Kuzmin; plug © Monkey Business Images; plumber © kurhan; plums © Valentyn Volkov; polar bear © Sergey Uryadnikov; popcorn, tissues © Vitaly Korovin; potato chips © a9photo; pretzels © Kesu; puppy © vgm; rabbits © camellia; rackets © spe; rhino © prapass; robot © charles taylor; rooster © Olgysha; rubber boots © Graphichead; rug © K. Miri Photography; rulers © photastic, nrt; salad © Subbotina Anna; sandals © FineShine; sandcastle © Becky Stares; sandwich, socks © Rafa Irusta; scarf, shirt © kedrov; scientist © mathom; seaweed © Kuttelvaserova Stuchelova; setting sun © Vibrant Image Studio; shark © Stubblefield Photography; sharpener © Gelpi JM; shed © Csaba Deli; sheep and her lambs © Eric Gevaert; shoe © WilleeCole; shoes © Nadezda Cruzova; shorts © John Kasawa; shorts © John Kasawa; skipping rope © feiyuezhangjie; slippers © marylooo; smiling little girl © Svitlana-ua; sneakers © Aleksandar Bunevski; soaps © Avdeenko, Bombaert Patrick; sofa © Mostphotos; spider © Kondor83; spinning top © Marek Szumlas; sponge © paranut; spring © Nixx Photography; star decoration © Jason Swalwell; stereo © Bombaert Patrick; stones © AlexussK; stool © Dan Peretz; strawberries © photastic; sunscreen © Lasse Kristensen; sweets, toy plane © design56; swimbands © Coprid; swimsuit © Ruslan Kudrin; t-shirt, dungarees, pyjamas © Irina Rogova; table © Simon Krzic; tablet PC © blinkblink; tambourine © grublee; tap © Roman Samokhin; Teddy © Kristina Postnikova; Telephone © spaxiax; tennis ball © DeanHarty; tights © Polryaz; tissues © Jami Garrison; tortoise, yellow tang © fivespots; towels © sagir, Sandra van der Steen; toy boat © Jiri Vaclavek; toy car © silvano audisio; toy teapot and cups © graja; toy tipper © photosync ; tricycle © Perutskyi Petro; Trumpet © bukinnet; tulip © Vasilyev ; ultralight © Meoita; underwear © Mitrofanova, Polryaz, Roman Sigaev; wafers © Polryaz, Roman Sigaev; waiter © mattomedia Werbeagentur; wardrobe © OZaiachin; wastepaper bins © humbak; watch © Skazka Grez; watercolour paint circles © donatas1205; wet dog © tkemot; wheelbarrow © digitalreflections; whisk © Bombaert Patrick; wildebeest © Gary C. Tognoni; windmill © Ramona Heim; window © Kristin Smith; wolf © Maxim Kulko; wooden spoon © Stephen Rees; wool © Nicku; xylophone © Olha Ukhal; yorkshire terrier © Vicente Barcelo Varona; yoyo © Olga Galkina.

Please note that every effort has been made to check the accuracy of the information contained in this book, and to credit the copyright holders correctly. Green Android Ltd apologize for any unintentional errors or omissions, and would be happy to include revisions to content and/or acknowledgements in subsequent editions of this book.

Printed and bound in China, October 2013

Note to parents and carers

Start to Learn Words is an exciting way to introduce your child to the world of words. Over 500 colourful photographs will encourage your child to browse through the book, recognising familiar items and discovering new ones.

Help your child build their vocabulary and learn vital reading skills by pointing to the clear labels as you name each of the pictures.

Designed as a fun learning experience, Start to Learn Words will entertain, as well as educate, young children for many hours.

Colourful photography of children

Clear labels

Challenging interactive questions

Contents

All about me

My body

face

Which child is the youngest?

hand

shoulder

arm

elbow

girl

hip

chest

leg

head

tummy

knee

tummy button

neck

back

ankle

toes

foot

baby

boy

heel

bottom

Which other parts of your body can you name?

My face

forehead

eyebrow

eye

ear

cheek

chin

What is the colour of your hair?

hair

eyelashes

nose

nostril

mouth

teeth

lip

Count the fingers on your hands.

My hands

palm

finger

knuckle

nail

wrist

thumb

My hair

straight hair

curly hair

long hair

short hair

My eyes

brown eyes

blue eyes

green eyes

What I wear

hoodie

dress

cardigan

What would you wear on your head?

leggings

boots

rain coat

jeans

woolly hat

belt

pants

trainers

Point to the stripy clothes.

socks

shirt

pyjamas

shorts

mittens

vests

skirt

Which of these clothes keep you warm?

tights

Which items do you wear on your feet?

dungarees

shoes

t-shirt

jacket

trousers

knickers

scarf

cap

earmuffs

watch

slippers

sandals

gloves

dressing gown

Find all the clothes with spots on.

rain boots

jumper

Food and drink

salad

juice

cereal

Point to the food you eat for breakfast.

sandwich

noodles

cakes

fruit salad

bagel

baked potato

crisps

pretzels

popcorn

rice

Which of these foods taste sweet?

yogurt

croissant

waffles

milkshake

bread

butter

Which of these foods is your favourite?

muffin

honey

boiled egg

toast

water

Which of these foods do you eat at a party?

cheese

nuts

pasta

ice cream

jam

pancakes

soup

sugar

doughnut

pizza

milk

chicken

chocolate

Can you count all the nuts?

chips

Colourful fruit

apples

pear

strawberries

watermelon

Which of these fruits is your favourite?

cherries

passion fruit

avocados

lemon

pomegranate

oranges

mango

blueberries

How many red fruits are there?

kiwi fruit

bananas

grapes

raspberries

plums

peach

pineapple

Tasty vegetables

cauliflower

cucumber

pumpkin

peas

How many carrots can you count?

aubergine

mushrooms

lettuce

sweetcorn

brussel sprouts

broccoli

tomatoes

potato

courgettes

Can you think of any other vegetables?

cabbage

onion

green beans

pepper

carrots

My home

window

pot plant

vase

pictures

vacuum cleaner

My family

father

mother

sister

brother

cat

computer

tablet

rug

bed

How many legs has the table?

door

stereo

telephone

sideboard

armchair

sofa

wardrobe

table

What colour is your front door?

drawers

lamp

television

In the garden

butterflies

hosepipe

kennel

dog

bush

trowel fork

gate

snail

shed

pots

wheelbarrow

earthworm

How many orange butterflies are there?

fence

grass

gardening gloves

ants

rake

flowers

broom

spider

watering can

ladybird

What might you keep in the shed?

In the kitchen

cooker

knife

fork

spoon

bowls

grater

How many wooden spoons are there?

pastry cutters

frying pan

saucepan

apron

toaster

refrigerator

colander

What do you like to cook?

plate

wooden spoons

stool

weighing scales

sink

oven glove

kettle

whisk

In the bathroom

tap

face cloth

toilet

toothbrush

tissues

toothpaste

What colours are the towels?

bubbles

plug

bath

bubble bath

hairbrush

soap

Which items are used on your hair?

towels

mirror

comb

toilet roll

nailbrush

shampoo

sponge

Toys

teddy bear

doll

cars

What colour is the truck?

guitar

skittles

How many farm animals are there?

playing cards

doll's house

dinosaurs

truck

spinning top

rocket

magnifying glass

trumpet

boat

modelling clay

toy spring

board game

dice

farm animals

What is your favourite toy?

tea set

binoculars

drum

xylophone

Which of the toys are vehicles?

tambourine

puppet

magnet

yo-yo

robot

cash register

toy money

marbles

tools

train set

jigsaw

building blocks

aeroplane

Which toys do you use to make music?

rubber ducks

At school

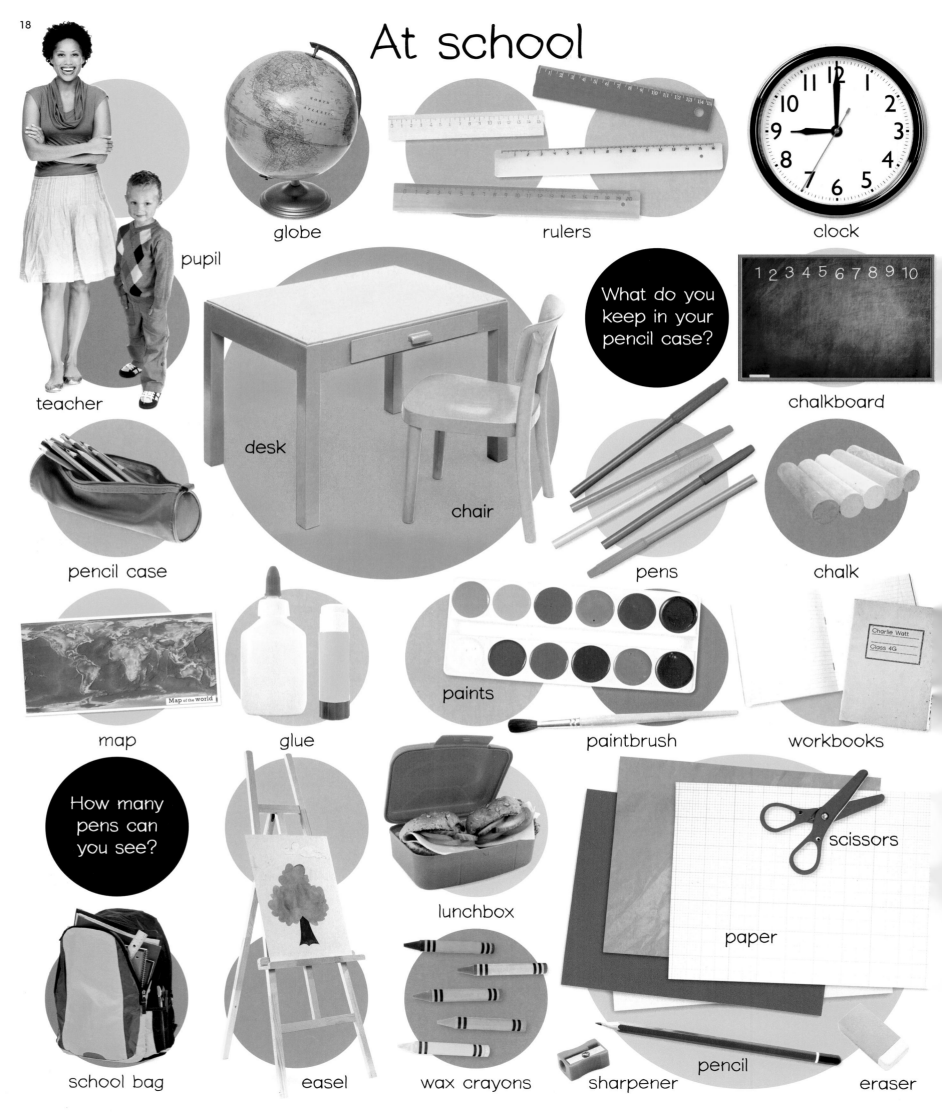

pupil

teacher

globe

rulers

clock

What do you keep in your pencil case?

chalkboard

desk

chair

pens

chalk

pencil case

map

glue

paints

paintbrush

workbooks

How many pens can you see?

lunchbox

scissors

paper

school bag

easel

wax crayons

sharpener

pencil

eraser

At the park

birds

trees

tricycle

skipping rope

inline skates

swing

slide

skateboard

sticks

balls

frisbee

bicycle

scooter

pond

rackets

pine cones

path

leaves

bench

Wild animals

panda

meerkats

shark

gazelle

owl

elephant

Which of these animals live in water?

sea lion

gorilla

hare

giraffe

zebra

penguins

tortoise

alligator

camel

crocodile

dolphin

Point to an animal with a hard shell.

brown bear

bison

Which wild animal is your favourite?

whale

eagle

lion

moose

koala

snake

chimpanzee

polar bear

frogs

kangaroo

Which animals have stripes on their coats?

hippopotamus

fox

wildebeest

wolf

rhinoceros

lizard

How many of these animals can fly?

tiger

cheetah

ostrich

People at work

scientist

Whose job is it to dance?

police officer

doctor   nurse

fire fighter

office worker

vet

Which job would you like to do?

football player   ballerina

waiter   chef

postal worker   pilot   mechanic   plumber   carpenter   builder   artist   musician

Time, the weather and seasons

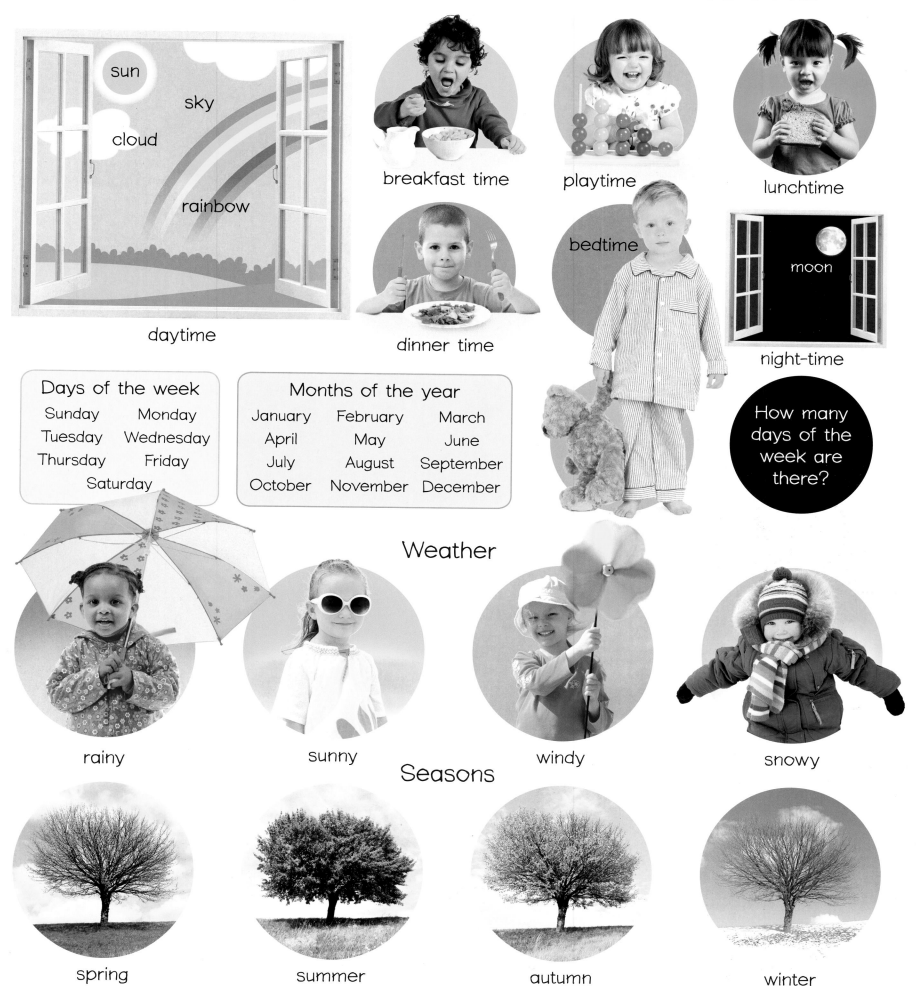

sun

sky

cloud

rainbow

daytime

breakfast time

playtime

lunchtime

dinner time

bedtime

moon

night-time

Days of the week
Sunday   Monday
Tuesday   Wednesday
Thursday   Friday
Saturday

Months of the year
January   February   March
April   May   June
July   August   September
October   November   December

How many days of the week are there?

Weather

rainy

sunny

windy

snowy

Seasons

spring

summer

autumn

winter

Which season has the warmest weather?

On the farm

horse

foal

goose

gosling

lambs

sheep

sheepdog

field

kid

goat

straw bale

What is a young goat called?

duck

duckling

plough

tractor

combine harvester

cow

calf

farmers

cockerel

hen

chicks

barn

turkey

piglet

pig

How many chicks can you find?

mouse

kite

sun cream

How many shells can you see?

bucket

spade

beach ball

camera

seagull

umbrella

deck chair

shells

sea

crab

ice lollies

What food do you like to eat on a beach?

swimming trunks

starfish

sandcastle

swim ring

beach bag

armbands

windmill

swimsuit

seaweed

sun hat

sand

On the move

ship

dump truck

compact car

dragster

hot-air balloons

glider

jet ski

microlite

digger

Which of these vehicles travels on water?

passenger train

hot rod

scooter

racing truck

jeep

limousine

ambulance

What colour is the hot rod?

hovercraft

go kart

Which of these vehicles would you like to ride in?

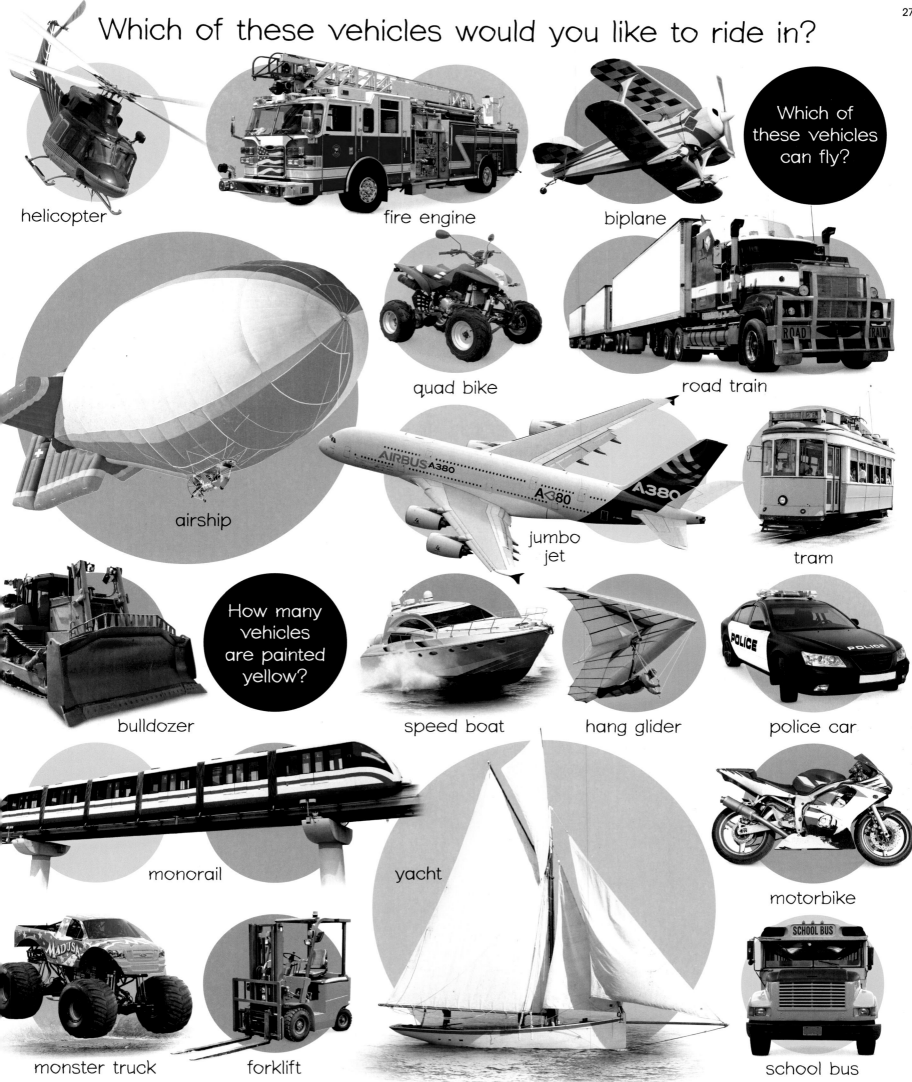

helicopter

fire engine

biplane

Which of these vehicles can fly?

quad bike

road train

airship

jumbo jet

tram

How many vehicles are painted yellow?

bulldozer

speed boat

hang glider

police car

monorail

yacht

motorbike

monster truck

forklift

school bus

Numbers
Can you count from one to twenty?

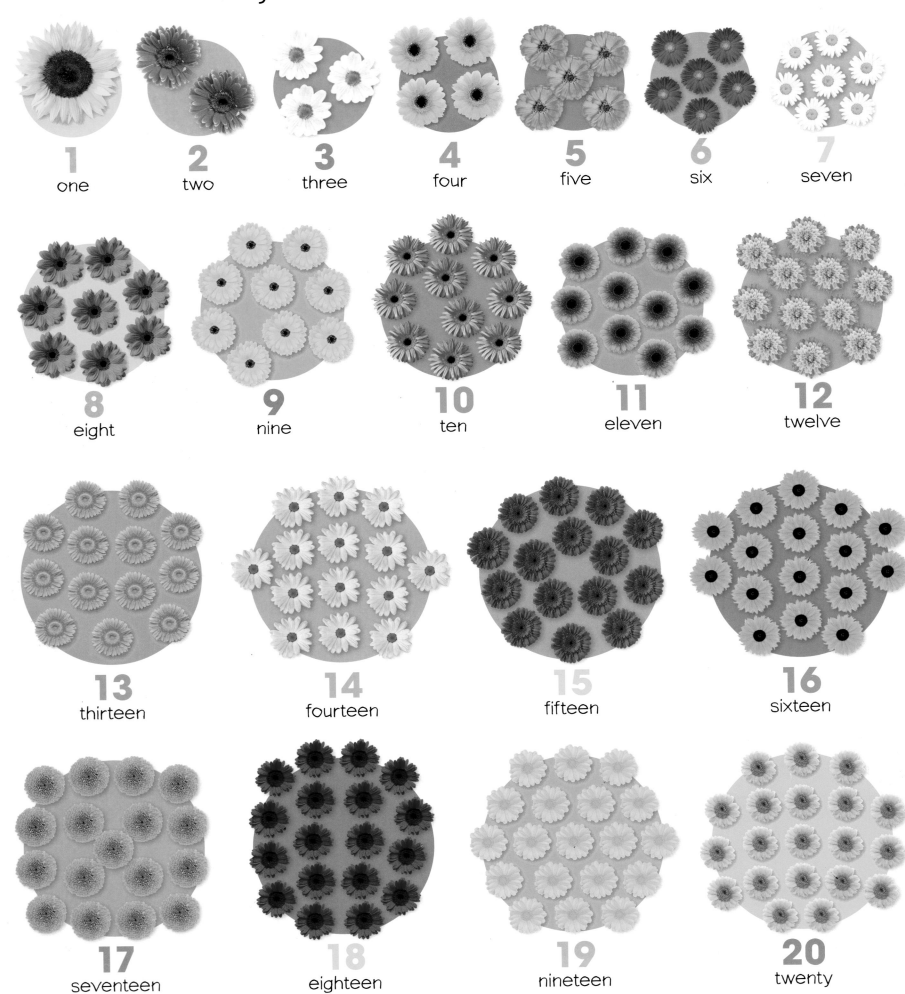

1 one

2 two

3 three

4 four

5 five

6 six

7 seven

8 eight

9 nine

10 ten

11 eleven

12 twelve

13 thirteen

14 fourteen

15 fifteen

16 sixteen

17 seventeen

18 eighteen

19 nineteen

20 twenty

Colours

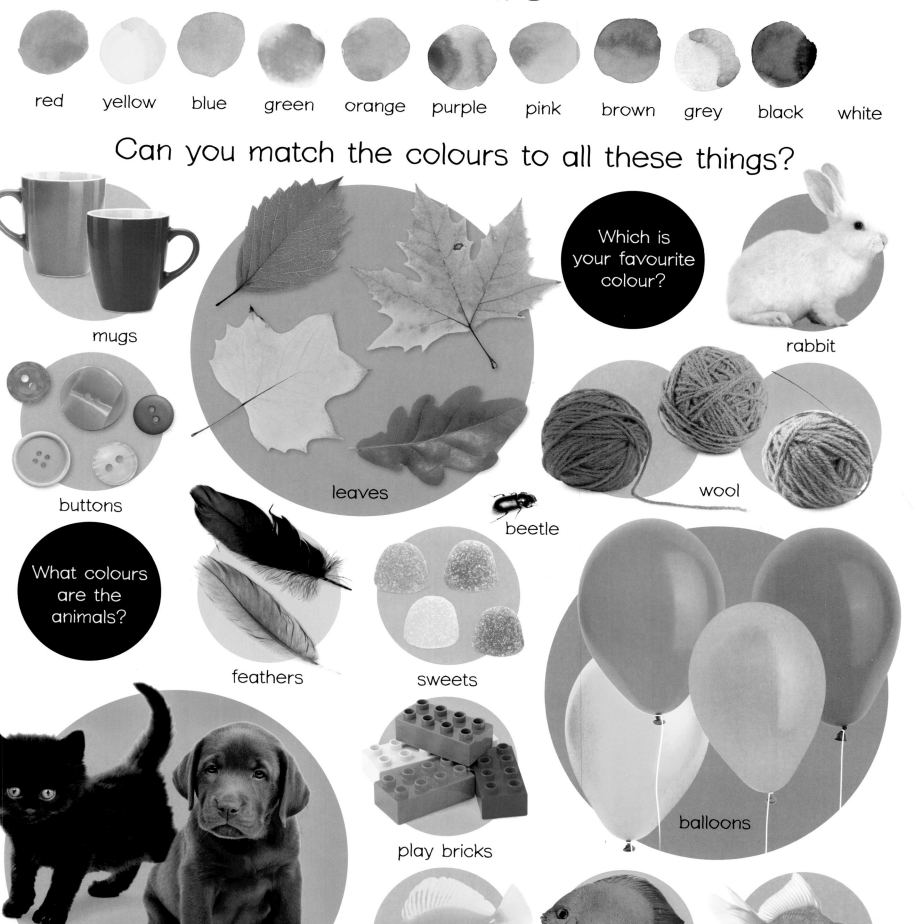

red yellow blue green orange purple pink brown grey black white

Can you match the colours to all these things?

mugs

leaves

Which is your favourite colour?

rabbit

buttons

wool

beetle

What colours are the animals?

feathers

sweets

balloons

kitten

play bricks

puppy

fish

Shapes

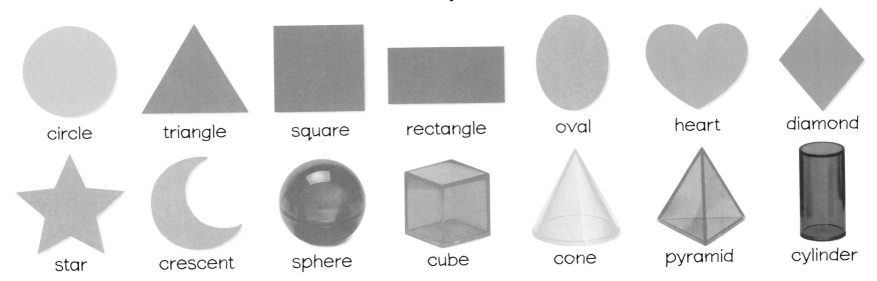

circle triangle square rectangle oval heart diamond

star crescent sphere cube cone pyramid cylinder

Can you name the shapes of all the objects below?

hanging decorations

candles

balls

How many triangles can you find?

cookies

envelope

pebbles

party hats

sunglasses

cushion

What shape are the pebbles?

bunting

road sign

Opposites

front

back

hard

soft

open

closed

heavy

light

clean

dirty

hot

cold

Where is the soft teddy bear?

long

short

wet

dry

old

new

happy

sad

high

low

full

empty

rough

smooth

thick

thin

How many building blocks are there?

small

big